*At Andy's*

# AT ANDY'S

*George Stanley*

NEW STAR BOOKS

VANCOUVER

2000

New Star Books Ltd.
107 - 3477 Commercial Street
Vancouver, BC V5N 4E8
www.NewStarBooks.com

Cover designed by Val Speidel
Cover image by Adad Hannah
Typeset by New Star Books
Printed & bound in Canada by Transcontinental Printing & Graphics
1 2 3 4 5   04 03 02 01 00

Publication of this work is made possible by grants from the Canada Council, the British Columbia Arts Council, and the Department of Canadian Heritage Book Publishing Industry Development Program.

CANADIAN CATALOGUING IN PUBLICATION DATA

Stanley, George, 1934 —
  At Andy's

  Poems
  ISBN 0-921586-76-0

  I. Title.
PS8587.T3232A72 2000          C811'.54          C00-910586-7
PR9199.3.S7A72 2000

*For my dear brother, Gerald, with love and admiration*

75

# Contents

# The Puck

skids on the ice (practically no friction). Sometimes it rolls —
then it's harder to whack into the net. We follow it. 'Watch Bure,'
Daniel says. 'Don't watch the puck — it'll come to him. 'I watch
the puck, the black dot. On the replays, of near goals, sometimes
I lose it, in the collision of bodies, the goalie spreadeagled, the
glare. Then it reappears. Is it in or out?

Second period. Somebody lights a joint. Now it's different.
Watch the puck *for dear life*. The puck *is* life — is like a word, in
conversation, the huge surrounding fucked reality — sense of
your own body, hunched, & the city, doomed — a terror —
where to fall would be to escape it, but you can't fall, you're
doomed, sentenced —

Somebody says something — but before the second word can
open its damp wings in the sunlight, there's a commercial, cars
or beer are pushed in your face,
                    but you can take it, you're
committed now (it's somehow like being a Red Crosse Knight
in the service of Una), as you watch the puck, that has its own
life among the players, in the game (that is worth the candle),

& all about the *cliffs of fall* — smoking dope it's like that's all
there is — the fall you can't fall, because you remember yourself
& forget the puck, the word,

& then you truly can't fend off the commercials, the car drives
into your head & is wedged there, & the beer pours through
your veins —

You are like Prometheus on the rock, & the car, the TV set with
a car for a head, the pterodactyl, is eating you, & you can't fall.

Third period. Now the beer is heavy in your brain & the dope
keeps calling you back to your damned self. Nonetheless you
know what you must do, keep your eye on that skittering black
blur, on what is between us & has its own life —

For when you think of nothing,
it gets by you, you miss the pass

✳

The word — the butterfly — its path — its road — depending
on so many — in the ambient — in the ambience — winged —
when it is set free, from the lips, we (who hear it) are set free,
from ourselves, to follow it — for courtesy — not *out of* courtesy,
but *in* courtesy — taking part — taking *parts*, as in song
                                                            When
no one is saying anything everyone is lapsed, fallen, into his own
inertia — sitting at the table, whirling around the sun —

In the beginning was the word — a definition of eternity —
                                                    & so
that's why you can't interrupt (Dale berated me in cold anger at
the first Adad salon, 'So you want to interrupt do you, you have
to say something do you, so say what you have to say,' & when I
said I'd quite forgotten, tried to pass it off, fiercely, 'No, say it!')
because the word has just begun its ascent,
                                        & promises to take

us, carefree, with it, & our own words can leap up & play with it,
so long as they don't injure it
                              but to interrupt is fatal, it's like a
plane crash. The word is eternal but it can be killed, like Jesus.

The puck is different. You can't cross
the river         you can't cross
the blue line         ahead of the puck

                              ✳

Decentered — the word is like some never-before-observed
beast — though you can't observe the word, you can hear its
whirring —
                the one who speaks the word — who *first* speaks it,
is he its creator? or only one who finds it — lost in time —
restores it to its birthright? — but it had its birth elsewhere —
the little child.

For the word to — the word is innocent, like the child — Bowering
wrote of the poem as *boy* — for the word to fly — eternally —
like the puck — it must be spoken by one of us — set free —
                                                            so
while our minds (for their own sake) are on the word — our
hearts go out to the speaker — she — who put herself on the
line — the blue line — risking the slow whistle —

                              ✳

The puck has to be kept in play. The puck is only a round of
hard rubber — a black bologna — frozen
                              doubly frozen, when
trapped against the boards by skates or sticks, or under the
sprawled torso of Kirk McLean, out of sight. The ref has to put it
back in play, at the face-off, drops it. The two players whack at it

— off it goes — that is what makes hockey the kind of game it is.

Thomas lights a joint. It is late in the third period, the Canucks are behind the Islanders or the Blues by 2 or 3 goals. Suddenly I am centered again. I am the puck (as Barry became the Centre, for a terrible moment.) It is all about *me* — history, this moment — the other players (what do I mean, 'other'?) are frozen ghosts — unless one whacks me with his stick — but inside me, there are players, too, whacking me, as I go skidding down the ice of time. What a story! How to escape it!

✳

How to escape being the focal point of history. Each one is stripped, like Jesus, of his garments, the cloth that tied him to the others. How to keep the others from fading. Our hearts go out to you for your willingness to speak — to be willing but not to will — to be on the lip of — the cataract — to be spring — where what was frozen can melt — where the child can appear —

the child the word the bird the butterfly the puck. They have no need of us. They keep repeating (unless the entire system of our love closes down, leaving us only these games —

But where our care does go, where it is wanted with a chemical hunger, is the willing, dying, speaker

# Dream of James Liddy, August 20, 1994

A wall burst into flame.

You were there, with the children in the basement.
One of them said: 'A bee-ship!' I knew that meant

souls were arriving

## Naked in New York

Ralph Macchio kissing Eric Stoltz on the lips, impulsively,
on the screen at the Hollywood. In the audience loud gasps,
as-if-sickened groans. These goofs must have known
their arrant discourtesy — o not to us,

but to *them*, the two giant heads soft as flags
or luminous clouds above us negotiating
a moment of intimacy — Macchio ruddy-cheeked,
        high on his cupid daring,
Stoltz (the beloved) cool, 'vanilla pudding' (Spicer) —

two Harvard boys at an arty New York party,
the straight one mildly pissed at being hit on — wanted,
but gratified by the compliment paid to his beauty
(not cataloguing the gay one's pain at his coolness),

but the guys in the seats, beneath them, the offended,
*not* wanted — outside this story — outside *Hollywood* —
this Harvard boy, really the actor Eric Stoltz,
rich, young, handsome, wanted,
& they not.

A boy being kissed by another boy could tip over the applecart,
all the shiny red apples in stacks, pyramids, buffed up for sale,
that were once in the dark of the barrel, homophobia high school,
hoping none of us was rotten, no bad apple, no queer,
certain we were all unwanted, none wanted by any of the others —
tipped over, apples rolling, bumping, bouncing, in the street,
    in the mud,
bruises, kisses (like pool balls), bites,
desire all over the place.

# Ars Poetica

A poem
should have the aplomb

of Kathleen Turner
in *Serial Mom.*

# Abner

'I'd trade places with him in a minute,'
said the young monk, of the chocolate-speckled
Catahoula hound rolling at his feet.

'You don't think much of being human,' said the old fox.
'No, I don't. You do, but you're an artist. Without art,
you're an animal.' And was out the door, dog at heels.

That hound is Abner.  He lives at the monastery
with four other dogs, one a white, female boxer pup
with a brown eyepatch, the other three bipeds — monks —
& Abner sniffs them all every morning
to know them — sometimes several times in one morning.
(It's not just recognition, there's more novelty in it —
as there is in the morning.)
                             Meanwhile the rain — the hail —
of information continues. The monks sit at the kitchen table,
reading the *Globe & Mail*. It tells them
how stupid they are not to understand
their true nature. 'Born to compete, boys.'
('Born to lose,' say the monks.) 'It's not just
the bondholders have you by the short hairs,
it's your attitude.'
                 If the *Globe & Mail*
could be translated into doggish, would Abner wonder,

'Compete? for food? for love?' Abner fights
with Dess, the boxer, for chewtoys, tug-of-war
with the old mophead, but that's just play,
not dog eat dog.

The monks compete. They compete with monks
from other monasteries.

The dogs howl when they're gone —
howl with loneliness. They don't know what time it is.

Hours, days, months, centuries pass.
Then suddenly the door opens. Ecstatic,
the dogs leap up, try to climb the monks,
lick their faces. Abner is so happy he wags his tail
so hard there are blood spots the whole length of the hall,
Abner-height.

The young monk talks to him.
'If my arms were forelegs, if my hands were paws,
I'd drop to the ground & be a dog like you,
I'd sniff the world.'
                        (But whose world would it be?
the old fox thinks, emerging from his den.)

'But you'd just like to be up here, reading the paper,
eating your dinner with a knife & fork,
& talking away, like me.'
                        The fox thinks
it's not exactly the moment to defend
humanity, or the dog's dim desire
to escape eternity, such as it is,
when he himself has been drinking whiskey
& reading philosophy, to get down.

# The Power of the Unhappy People

The unhappy people have great power.
They invest in the unhappiness of others.

Not generic unhappiness, the kind
of unhappiness anyone could feel,
but designer unhappiness, the exact
shape of the hole in your heart.

These are dreams without doors. Let the blonde
demonstrator slip one around your feelings.
As it goes on, it clings like shrink-wrap.

Now the birds can cry in the night, and you
won't hear them. Or your ancestors. Or jazz.
The image of your death will dance for you
with as many veils as you please.

In your fog-coloured room, in your Queen Anne chair,
you may wish you were dead, but be glad of that wish
since it sets you above the common sort
inured to ordinary unhappiness.

And we, the investment community, will grin.

(Though like you, we cannot feel the sun or hear the rain.
Or jazz.) We will grin at the thought of you dreaming.

More & more people must become rich & unhappy,
so the original unhappy people can die rich.

# The Wasteland (A Translation)

I'm going to tell you a story —
but it's not really a story —
it's not all in the past —
it's happening now.

On a fall evening, in the outskirts of Moscow,
I was walking alone down a little path
through a wasteland. I heard
voices, singing. Then I saw them,
a noisy gang, five or six young guys,
apparently drunk, shouting a song.
No way to turn back, to run away in shame.
I kept walking towards them,
gripping my keys in my pocket,
thinking, no good will come of this.

Then I recognized the song — they were singing
'Toum-Balalaika,' or trying to sing it,
in Yiddish, like Jews. One young man
knew the verse, the others came in on the chorus:
'Spiel, Balalaika, Toum-Balalaika!' I felt relieved.
I remembered that this was a holy day for the Jews,
and here were our Judaizing Russian youth, singing
after synagogue. No harm from them.

'Shalom, guys,' I said, & they, all in chorus,
replied, 'Shalom, grandpa!'

They backed off, & I went on my way
filled with sad thoughts.
Not because they had called me grandpa
(though it did seem a little early for that)
but because I asked myself:
How have we come to the point
where a Russian, an Orthodox Christian,
has to be afraid of young Russians,
but not of those who would call themselves Jews?

Then another thought: Young people, will you leave this
    country?
It is not a bad country. We could share it with you.
The ones I had feared to meet tonight,
they are not going anywhere, who would take them?
But you will probably go, and then the chance
that my next meeting with strangers, in the wasteland at night,
will be an unpleasant one, that chance
will have increased, greatly.

Young people, don't leave!
Look, I will plant trees in this barren place.
We will start our lives again.
You are ours, you are Russians like us.
What matter who our ancestors were,
Slavs, Swedes, Finns, Turks or Jews.
Alexander Pushkin himself belongs to all of us,
whose grandfather was an Ethiopian,
& his grandmother German, from Estonia.

But those who for ten years now
with the methodical passion of drunks
have broken the glass panes
of the bus shelter in our street
(glass panes replaced no less methodically
by the municipality of Moscow)
them I don't consider Russians,
even if their names were Popov
three times over. They don't love this land,
it is alien to them. It would be better if they
would leave Russia & go live somewhere …
in the Soviet Union.

But as for Boris Finkelstein,
with whom I have planted birch trees in the wasteland,
to make more beautiful, as best we could,
this corner of our poor Russia that we share,
I think that there is no one more Russian than he.
And I don't want him to leave,
for without him there will be
fewer birch trees here. Fewer still,
since our 'Soviet' drunks keep breaking the saplings
and each spring we have to plant new ones.

*Adapted from the Russian of Arkadi Tcherkassov*
*through the French of Lionel Meney*

# A Man

*for Meredith Quartermain*
*in response to 'The World'*

The cup didn't break (I prefer to think),
only jumped, jiggled, when his fist hit the fake
woodgrain table, as did a couple of pencils,
a plastic ballpen, a paper clip. 'Shit,' he said.
To no one.

Fragments of a thought. Age, experience, destiny.
But strike that last one, for one who believes the universe
has no purpose, he has no purpose, walked
(well, stepped, a foot or two, in an eight-foot cube)
to where the windows ought to be, & stared.

The mountains have some kind of eternal — rejected
several complements, majesty, bare quality, finally
settled on aura, he mused, at least to those
who call them mountains. The earth is as smooth
as an orange, said the devil. He let that one
go by. They were gods, or the habitations of gods,
so we (thinking, men) could crawl between earth
& heaven, at least that.

Sky gods, she said, looking up from the stack of papers
she was marking. So that was out, too, taking refuge
in stories. The whole stratification slipped,
towards the intertidal zone, the female soup.

I could identify with my breath, he thought.
This skin, this lexicon, but a bag, the eternal
pastry tube ...

# Outside the Kingdome

Outside the Kingdome a guy with a UCLA
Bruins T-shirt & a cap of some other team
wants to be part of it. This big vacant space
we've come to love because it gives us vantage.

How to cheat Death except to build Hell
outside its gates, after the game.
The ticket stubs & other stuff
blown idly about, by the teenage wind.

# Terrace '79

Driving up into hills of fall,
mottled yellow & red,
or hills of spring, with friends *still young* —
col*leagues*, Peter said, accenting the second
syllable,

that would read together,
look out on the land,
referred to a world long gone
as if that were the world, and this,
on the Skeena, an adventure. *Colleagues.*

Watching us were adult children
of Ontario settlers, whose people
had made a clearing in the bush
by the train track, around 1912.
People with plain churches & unvarnished ideas,
or ideas the varnish had weathered off —
a fine dust of predestination.
Their backyards abutted
on feral orchards.

Watching them were the numerous people
living in the bush, dark & horned.

Hard to see at first, but then apparent
all at once, like berries.

We rode up & down the river, we chartered planes
& sent the bills some place called budget.
We imagined ourselves at the frontier
of the imagination (last days of we).

Terrace was New York of the North — after hours on the road,
a scatter of white lights, dim bulb over the motel doorstep,
quartz halide at the freightyards.

The scientists (Allen & Ian) stepped off the road,
walked up the mountains, waded into the river
(bought hip boots, borrowed canoes
& Zodiacs). Fished,
& up came the fish,
the students, bounding upstream,
up the streams of our ironizing minds,
or idled in the shallows
*eddying* (Dora's word), to gain strength.

We still young, academic dreamers & misfits,
led their children into the forests of meaning.
Most would go part way only, not intrepid as we
(whose life support came from general revenues of BC),
then run back to the highway, charmed by the blacktop that led
to parking lots & venues of advancement ...

# Family Eyes

Whether by blood or mere authority,
this knowledge: eyes look out of an awful
lostness.
      Lost & found on earth, together.

The eyes of friends are beautiful jewels.
The eyes of lovers are perilous mirrors.
Family eyes scope the skulking soul.

# In Scotland

Necropolis behind
Glasgow cathedral,

Scottish boys
with soft close cuts.

# Return of the Abbot

*for Leo*

'The monastery cannot be destroyed,' said the abbot.
'I have planted a dogwood tree. It is illegal
to cut down dogwood trees. Therefore, the monastery cannot be
    destroyed.'

'I didn't bother to tell him,' said Fra Pietro,
'that in two years his dogwood tree will still be a sapling, not very
    tall.
The new owner will have it dug up & wrapped,
with the dirt clinging to its roots & some added dirt,
in burlap, & hand it to the abbot, saying:
'Here's your tree. Now get the fuck off my land.'

The abbot returned home on Sunday.
He brought a bottle of Jameson from the duty free shop in
    Amsterdam,
& gathering about him the monks, friends & supporters
    of the monastery, in unsolemn conclave,
they drank the Jameson, & two cases of beer,
& the abbot smoked a pack of cigarettes, & two joints,
& made about thirty phone calls. And when everybody had left,
    or gone to bed,
the abbot cleaned up the kitchen.

Today, the abbot, being 'without wheels,' left on the stagecoach
for 41st & Arbutus, to drop in on the landlords.
The abbot is chairperson of the tenants' committee.
(The monastery is only one of several tenants in this 1920s-era
    corner retail-residential property, others being a hairdresser,
    'retro' furniture store, art students, etc.)
No formal election was held for this post.
Everyone knows the landlords
expected the return of the abbot
& knew the committee would not be formed
until he came back.

Now, in the middle of the night, the abbot
enters the monastery again,
festooned with 12-packs. Behind him,
dark against the dark, the bowed heads of two


novices.

# Dobie (shot for poaching)

Fierce & independent as a wolf,
courteous as an urbanite,
your silence resembled the human silence
of a sea captain or explorer,
one who had seen much in more than one world.

# Fox on the Seabus

Seeing a small boy lay his head upon
his father's knee & go off for a nap,
the fox has a *mémoire involontaire*, he recalls

how he, a child, had more than once shut eyes
& fallen asleep (& smiled in sleep, he thinks)
amid adult ado, & dreamed his dream.

It is allowed, Fra Giacomo has said,
more than once, in the monastery,
as if stating a general law.

# Aubade

*for Reg*

I was dreaming of my death when a car
alarm woke me. The odor of the dream
stayed in the room.
                    I tried to think
of some distraction: bodies of my former
lovers gone missing. The previous day
had vanished, too. Thoughts of the one to come
pulsed in my brain like bells in a poem
by Poe.
        Then my eye lit upon
the rosy numerals of the bedside clock: 4:30.

4:30 — is 43 times 10.
4:31 — is prime. 4:32 ...

& sleep came back, on mathematical sails.

# The Ripple

It's all me.

I can say that without any thought of an image of
our separateness or a thought of an imageless    As it all comes
    back,

it sticks, it becomes
me, like candy.
And I'm alone        I don't know what to do        I turn into myself,
take it all (the world)
and glove it        out of sight        The world remains        a tear,
through which I dying see
the world, relieved of tension
and simple        simple as a leaf.        And it is there and I can
    step up

into it        and use it again        It is new

Soon it becomes all me again.        Then I die again with the
    pain of
my fingernails, my cock, my toes, my eyes
to still it        It won't go away.        It still remains, its wave,
    its constant ripple, closing in

(I had dinner at the East-West house last night, and met this guy,

Tom, wavy dark hair, mustache, Italian or Jewish I guessed, about my age, I could see dark chesthair curling at his throat, over his T-shirt. Once he asked me about poetry. After dinner we got stoned: Knute, Bill Reis, Tom and I. I asked Knute if he was going to walk to North Beach. Tom answered, said he was going to walk that way, so he could hitchhike to Berkeley off Broadway. Scared (in the easy chair, me, of unknown he, walking with him, talking to him. The late empty streets, the dark hills, with — forgot his name. Sneaked a glance over at him on the couch, dark eyes, mustache — Who is he? I don't know him. Scared went away, found the Tao again

(As it happened, Knute did walk over. Tom and I and Knute walked down Bush St., I was in the middle

(From maybe twenty years in the future I looked back on this. Sneaked a glance at Tom again, walking next to me on Bush St., and realized: I never knew him. He was a friend of Bill Reis's, used to come over to the East-West house a lot. I never knew him at all. I *recognized* him

(We walked to North Beach, talking about architecture. When we got to Broadway & Columbus, Tom said goodnight, and he said to me, 'Maybe next time we can talk about poetry.' 'O.K.' Then Knute and I went to the bar.

(Twenty years in the future I was sitting on the edge of my bed in a hotel room in Montreal, examining my hands. There was late afternoon light. The shade was kind of pushed into the room by the warm air but didn't move. Looking at the little moles on my skin      It was all me. There had never been any other. Had been no one else. Faces, what dreams, I laughed or remained silent because they

laughed or remained silent. And now not they. Me
on the bed, and it
hanging off there

with no mind of its own

world

*San Francisco 1970*

# Ripple +26

*For Ken Bullock & Philip O'Connor*

26, not 20. Years. In the future. I'm sitting on the edge of my bed
in a hotel room in Montreal, yes, but not examining my hands,
the spots of age are there, yes, but I have no wish to examine any
part of me, wish, I wish, no wish. In San Francisco I thought, & I
don't care what I thought, I looked forward, I imagined, to this
moment, 20, only it's 26, years, to ratify (whatever that means,
turn into a rat, I guess) some notion I had of me (& the rat's
loose now, behind the boards).

This is an old Victorian, a *manoir* it's called (now I have to shift
over, on the bed, writing (& see my 62-year-old legs) (what was
so important about not remembering someone's name (I *still*
forget people's names when I get stoned) that it took me 26 years
to (I'm sitting in a hotel room in Prince George trying to
remember what it was so important to remember in a hotel
room in Montreal about not remembering someone's name in
San Francisco 26 — I forget. And the guy whose name I forgot
— Tom? — now I've forgotten *him*, though Monday (last
Monday (2 Mondays ago) in Vancouver, Ken Bullock told me
Phil O'Connor had been asking after me, & that's longer, 47
years I guess since I've seen him, he was one of my moral
mentors (*one* of?) I told Ken, taught me something about lust for
power, i.e., you don't pick on 3 guys (pages, at the Main Library

- 31 -

(Kelham, 1917), when there's 9 of you (even if you are a sissy) —
but me, me, that's important (the rat sd), I meant that isn't
important (isn't it nice the way he cleans the blood off his hands
before dinner (& twisted another way, so now he could see he
was wearing paisley shorts, tapered boxers ('You refuse to get old'
— B.G.) — I'm not as old as this *manoir* — I lost it.

It doesn't matter where you start or where you end, you're you
(I'm you), not me, there is no rat (not so fast, you want to get
your thoughts together, like candy eggs (the colours of the 4
Montreal subway — *métro*! — lines — blue, orange, green,
yellow — in an Easter basket (& back there in San Francisco
there was something about candy too — let's face it (he sat up &
faced it — curtain, window, lightwell, highrise — a false note

I'm sitting on the edge of this bed in a Montreal hotel room &
there is nothing that needs to be said (o false note of closure —
thanks, sd the rat, I have lots to say, & I'm driving (there is no
rat)

I read poetry last night to 6 people — 3 seemed interested — not
including me — I do this for myself. I'm sweating all over. I'm
wearing weird brown socks (or are they gold?) with black &
white squares on them. I don't want to deny what the guy 26
years back said — he said 'It's all me' — it was all him — sure,
the world has no mind — no one mind — there is no 'world' —
now that's a fact — or the lack of a fact. It isn't candy — is that a
rat running cross the roof? He jumped up, pulled back the
curtain all the way, looked out — it looked back, from up on the
fire escape — no, not a rat, a white squirrel. Now that certainly
ain't part of me, a coloured Easter egg.

Those 3 guys we were going to beat up, or 'get' in some way, were library pages. Phil was one of them — the biggest one — & he came & said to me (we were standing in the doorway of the little anteroom behind the main reading room, where we pages sorted books & put them on trucks for shelving) — 'What if it had been Ken?' (another Ken — a smaller boy — & he'd be over 60 now (the rat is wearing a yellow shirt — the one I wore last night at the reading — purple tie, check — & driving, driving — forget the rat). That was the first time I heard moral indignation in anyone's voice. Christ, I didn't want to hear that. That we tune out (what was so important to remember, I didn't remember someone's name? For a minute. A minute or 2. And then the Tao came back, I wrote then. I don't think I've got my thoughts very well organized here. Not like those beautiful rubber-tired subway cars.

I guess I'll just have to keep driving — writing. I guess I am the rat (ratified, finally) sitting on the real bed in the real hotel room in the real Montreal, with my half-eaten candy thoughts, & always the sickness of incomplete — just wanting to locate myself here as you rather than me. You know, Emily Carr said when the dark asked her why. You know. You Who Know (Nicolas Freeling) wanting to disappear, of course, but be here, if it takes all night, if it takes 26, 47, 62 years to put lust for power behind me.

*Montreal / Prince George 1996*

# Sex at 62

*for R.*

His head bent toward me, he demanded,
'Lots of kissing, when I make love' — I could
let my mouth be devoured, I could be held —
back & forth rocking, from being held —
& his arms, his hands, all over my body,
admiring its smoothness. I said, no, yours
is smoother, mine is horny, scaly as a
reptile — it was in these moments of talk,
a gift, a joke, the rocking stopped —
we were falling (through the bed
it seemed, the drugs were wearing off),
into some kind of knowledge, unspoken,
this physical syntax —

I knew him, then all through the morning
as we sucked & kissed & caressed
that it was him, got ahead of
this jerky demanding need to *do*
sex, when it was him there was no choice,
only a face, his rough chin, tousled hair —
then we sat in the Naam eating cereal,
his face & neck white, & the black overcoat.

The fear & the demand, to *make* love,
are still here, but the mythology is gone —
the fear & the demand weaker, & desire
weaker — but that it is him, that is
stronger, that the night lit up from inside
the cab when my arm turned his not-
unwilling face to me & the body answered —

he was (is) connected to the night, the city —

The cock is a torch, a light,
that lights up the body & our bodies light up
the night —
                    I can see the end
through him as I kiss him goodbye
at the bus stop, but the face & the words
& that it is him, that shines —

What else — oh that he was Stephen & I
Leopold & the hours were also rooms —
the bar & the taxi on Hastings & the bedroom —
lighted — moving (losing it, touching,
knowing, losing it

towards the mouth, mouth on mouth,
        the mouth warm wet,
dark red the lips around, the dots
of beard, the eyes that would suddenly
open to see me & seductively close,
        deluxe,
the lighted-up minutes, desire breaking
through fixations, making me
glad I'm old, glad they don't hold

no more, letting him, body against mine,
turning & turning over — but going
too fast — doing too much too fast — not
loving the time, slower, better next time

never get any closer

# At Andy's

*for Andy and Martina*

Terrace '97. I arrive here on the bus, Andy & Martina pick me
up (while I'm writing I'll try to ignore undercurrents of the
brain, personal worthiness, outcome or 'point' of this writing,
e.g., or should I include them? A pointless paragraph. I can't
write.

OK, I guess I really do have to freewrite & quit fucking around.
So — dive in — splash — *in medias res* — don't like this pen,
point too short — I arrive on the bus — strip mall on Keith —
we stop at Safeway for groceries — obesity — almost everyone
too big, I think, is the weight of all the food that gets here, by
truck (less waste, and, Andy reminds me, heat loss) added to the
bodies of those living here, Terraceites?

Streets jammed with cars, we take the long way up to the bench,
a kid pulling away from the West Side food store drinking a
Coke seems enclosed in his car — encased —

What's wrong is somehow I think there's something to write
*about* — instead of writing.

I'm sitting down here in Andy's basement at Vicky's old desk on
a hot Sunday in August thinking I should write about

something, or rather, that I should (emphasize *should*) write (emphasize *write*) to justify my existence — my life — to myself (& then having justified self, I can be with others, have a drink with Andy, e.g., without feeling self-unjustified (un-self-justified?). I'm appalled — horrified — that at age 63 I still think this way — write this way. I can't write, Barry & I say. What would 'writing' be? I think of the quick, sharp (objectivist) takes on heart & world in GB's 'Blondes on Bikes' — I can't do that — wouldn't even try, to act so nonchalant, i.e., pretend to. I started out to write about Terrace & here I am writing about myself, with as bad a fit between this so-called writing activity (free writing — what's *free* about it?) — & content — & poetry! — as ever. I should *pray*, I guess — just keep writing this silly shit & pray for a poem.

✳

White hair on the back of my hand — radio going upstairs — I go upstairs, Andy tells me about constant noise from next door subdivision — rottweilers, dachshund — bulldozer — angry crows. I go outside, sit on porch, hear crows —

I hear crows in Vancouver — I have nothing to write about, & am not in right state to dive deep — on edge here — hate this pen — there is no content — or is age content? (Kavanagh: 'they know it to a day') — fuck that — feeling myself breathe — insect makes wide sweep around flowerpot — Teddy barks —

Poetry means (a) I'm going to die — & (b) this notebook will be read by someone who will see how lacking I am — unless I destroy it — & I can't do that — that would be worse than keeping it — that would mean thinking of it. Better this shit than nothing, better be sitting on Andy's front porch with Teddy, imagining this shit being (miraculously) turned into a poem —

as Spicer said, not the Vietnam War but Autumn in Vermont —
a poem about obesity, cheerful obesity, all the big people
trundling their carts & bags of groceries out to their cars parked
at the mall — one lifestyle — nothing but the economy — the
drinking water sour — environmental movement focused on the
immediate, daily threats to health —

At the college — MACLABUSE, one word, becomes MACL
ABUSE, a new threat? Abuse, abuse, obese — truckloads of log
corpses from farther & farther away, up the Nass — operate the
mill at lower cost, develop the mining sector, truckloads of food
— this is a site of conversion, realization of surplus value, how
else to conceive of it.

No way to conceive of it, no understanding. And I'll never know
if it's really understanding that's disappearing or am I just
moaning the loss of a sharper mind.

Well, I've started writing again.

✳

Drinking water — foul — a sour or flat taste & then a chemical
aftertaste — two-stage foulness.

Sky overcast — air muggy — due to automobiles? Is anything
'natural' anymore?

This is not poetry. But what would a poem about Terrace be
like? Objective — at a distance from the mind, posing as
anybody's perception, idea — or no one's. The View from
Nowhere. But is there another alternative? Ah, inspiration!

I wish I had a desk — I'm sitting on this duvet in Annyha's

bedroom, balancing the writing book on my naked knees — I feel like I'm in the jungle. But nothing to pounce on me, except myself — always pouncing.

Fine rain, and now, to the west, a rift of blue like a river in the white cloud — blue rifts opening up over the cedars — fine rain — me here — a visitor — seeing Terrace from the outside. I was extracted — like a tooth — early retirement — & the skin of Terrace closed easily behind me, the placidity, the obesity. A feeling of contentment — & exclusion — at the edges of this the trees are eaten — the best logs hauled, the second best burned or buried — hauled back here — then the conversion begins — the logs turn into money (the computer watches the saw) — some of it stays here — & then the trucks come, the food — & also the car carriers (any name for that?), rattling & clanking, steel ramps, chains — an objective poem, no one's vision —

Cars moving slowly up Lakelse — cumbersome — in & out of parking spaces — slow — because so heavy & so dangerous — & there is food, in bags, in carts, lifted into trunks & back seats of cars, backs of pickups, in mall lot. Cars & trucks move slowly, heavily, towards the exit, then move like heavy tanks into the traffic lanes, & then, inside all this, inside the cars (the objective poem sees) there are people, placid, cheerful —

What a vision! — is there behind this some animus — is it deep dislike of these people, misanthropy, or just objective — is this a phenomenon anyone could observe or the twisted vision of a fucked-up old man — is there anything natural — or is it *all* natural — blameless — the programmed activities of sapiens with their tree trunks on trucks, wood chips in hopper cars, cars & carts & such no less than insects with sticks & leaves — each has its function, its social role.

The salt lost its savour, but is it only in my life? What is it I don't grant them, the Terraceites of '97 — the right to be fat & happy & to have overcome (not individually, but *en masse*), simply by not learning it, dread?

✳

Who can see the inner Terrace? Do our individual hearts meet there as our social selves meet here in this slow moving jumble of steel carapaces & Safeway carts & fat pleasant faces with the log trucks an undertone in the background? We aren't crowded together there, that I know. Or do we not meet? Is there a place, even in summer, where each man (& woman) moves continually *away*, through a personal winter, saying, 'this is true'?

There's no way to know except by knowing them, which here I don't, except my old friends — & their knowledge of each other, seen in faces & heard in tones of voice more than in words — knowledge of what is not said, out of kindness — life a condition of unsaying, of waiting for the unsaid to fade, of waiting for forgetfulness while preserving shards of memory, of avoiding laying it all on each other, out of forbearance.

In Hawthorne's story, *The Minister's Black Veil*, the minister blames his community for their forbearance as if that were a sin of secrecy & not a balm of love — to suffer the unsaid in privacy — in one's knowledge that ultimately that's what there is — aloneness — the urge to lay it all on the other being a desperate cry, a try, at leaping that bulwark of loneness, to enforce mutual knowledge, mutual terror.

Do we consume merely out of duty, is it a façade, that we pretend to savour the objects we devour, pretend to praise the process, and these fat smiles are not of satisfaction in consuming

but of living in virtue, of never revealing, of ever concealing, the
true life we know the other also lives — in darkness, in winter?

✻

(At Mr. Mike's)

I can't separate my feelings from their faces. If I could peel them
back like a film, from the fat & placid — huge man ordering
grapefruit juice — 'on a diet' — what would they seem?

They would seem nothing — their faces are in my mind —
that's not solipsism, just Terrace-ism. I sit in Mr. Mike's — the
veggie burger & Coke — a sketch in the brain —

✻

(On the Halliwell bus)

The bus driver said of one of his passengers: 'When she started
riding the bus she wouldn't say a word. You'd ask her a question
& she'd give you just a little short answer. But now …' (Pause.)
'She's a Christian, her parents brought her up to be a Christian
— but I told her, hey, I don't hold it against you, & she gave a
little laugh.'

By which they know how they feel — she knows he didn't mean
to dis her faith — but they say so little — 'she wouldn't say a
word' means a feeling that could be explained in other words,
shy, or frightened even, but the driver doesn't —

Maybe the bus driver knows why she wouldn't say a word —
abuse — but won't say, maybe because he's protecting her —
from a word, spoken out loud, to a stranger — to me — 'I
haven't seen you on this bus before' —

Feelings are there in the air, in the mind — 'this side of the grass' we walk among feelings — & carry feelings in our brains — & so the faces act as doors — set in lines — not to let words in. Words dart about inside, puckish — Andy's father asked what that word meant — mischievous, *méchant* — up to no good — words, like spirits, neither good nor evil, just natural — but some would call them good *and* evil — Christians — so the faces —

❋

Who am I, a ghost? Walking up from Greig to Lakelse — one of those streets east of Kalum — empty lots & broken house foundations — weeds — think, am I here — am I a ghost? I'm not here, not in the sense that thoughts & feelings & the odd word (at the joint — words at the joints) would carry me — to the next meeting — I could be going to a meeting (come in late, like Ken Belford) — for city politics or to get drunk or for sex — yes, many of those meanings — meetings — but no network —

& love & courage, Simon Thompson said, at the bar, at Hanky's — we had met there every year & now were meeting again — Rocque, José, Andy — those narratives, Simon said, are somehow replaced or annihilated — by consumer —

Happy to read an account of Margaret Laurence's suicide — her own account — she couldn't find the teakettle to heat the water to melt the Diazepam — tranquilizer, Andy says, like Prozac — so she used the coffeemaker, but didn't put any coffee — just hot water & Prozac — & the glinting memory — faces of joy — one last?

❋

Dream poem: tyler alters / night amber / with sensation.

❋

The same world for me as for Andy — we agree. Not the Thing-in-Itself — that horror-movie creature — but a thing between us and the Thing — something we have made up (using all our unspoken language) — call it world. So how is it I stand in it, on the broken asphalt & concrete sidewalks of Terrace, & feel it not — feel it *as* not — as departure, Rilke might say? At Andy's I feel part of it, hearing Andy's lawnmower, seeing the grey pile rug & blond dresser in Annyha's room, two pairs of my shoes — writing at 3:15 p.m. — it feels like I'm here, & that I won't leave.

The world that seems so frightening (admit it) when smoking dope (it's the fright I'm admitting, not the dope) or when thinking — too rationally — you could sit on the porch — *and* imagine it — stars coming on in the 10 o'clock evening, maybe Orion, time of year? — but chill, too early for stars to come out fully — late by the clock, but too early for the meteor shower — Andy's voice from the dark, down by the barn — 'take 15 or 20 minutes longer, but I'm not waiting, I'm going to bed.' 'Me too.'

Located in it — not located — in it — not in it — it — not it — I? — no, not I — the? The the (Barry's line, from Wallace Stevens). The with stars.

✳

Old Lakelse Lake Road — driving to John & Larisa's for dinner. I'm holding the dessert in my lap — a cake — & Martina in front of me holds a bowl of caramel sauce. Andy drives. Dark sky — scattered rain — second growth cedars packed in — roadside bushes — branches waving in the wind. I watch the raindrops crawl up the windshield & I feel the void, like a natural phenomenon, stabbing out of the clouds, or flashing without light — but alternating — on & off — with its absence — something more substantial? — faith?

## Men in Black

Exit the Cineplex Odeon, Prince George.
A sunny afternoon in August. A path
through four imaginary dimensions.

K turns his memory over to J — no,
K asks J to burn out his memory
(using a hand-held laser-like device)
of being ingested by a giant cockroach,
an alien trying to steal the galaxy —

K dove headfirst down the bug's gullet
to retrieve a favourite gun, then blew it up
from inside, thus spattering him & J
with fragments, guts & bug-goo —

& of other such adventures.


2

K's mission — the mission of the Men in Black —
was to keep the masses on Earth from noticing
they were menaced at every moment by aliens.
Now K seeks that oblivion for himself,

to return to the blameless masses,
be one of the extras. J freaks
when he begins to realize K
is taking himself out of the movie.

I would like to get off this path, find a gate
left open through some mistake of my own
into a flowering desert where nothing connects,
where each moment is one of recognition
& forgetting.

K will have to come out of retirement
(in the sequel). His gun will be
useless, in a world menaced
not by aliens, but by memories.

# Robson St. '97

On Robson planet, you have the right
to place your foot, well shod —

The madman recites the words of a song
in a horrible voice & stops walking, stops short,
to make his mad point, that the walkers are thoughtless —

It's not a stroll, or a *paseo*, it's a
determined pace, they pass each other up,
the boys in muscle shirts walk three abreast —

They're on their way to the very near future,
the rainbow veil, when the street & all its people
resolve into a phrase, or a fashion,
something that is happening everywhere,
but also not happening —

happy without happening. No country for old men
hiding in their T-shirts — all this summer —
summer on Robson St. — yet cold
& without passion — without person —

the condition of the beach resort
brought to centre city — bodies full of meaning —
police on horses —

Long past the documentaries.

# Sun & Rain

*for Jay*

Sun and rain.
Turmoil in my heart.

You are distant, like the sun.
And close as rain is cold.

Sun and rain.
Turmoil in my heart
(when you read my horoscope).

Sun:
    distant
    and hot.

Rain:
    The rain in your heart
    wets me.

    The rain in your heart
    wets me.

# Outside Golden

Uncanny — waves of rock — leaning north —
above forest — sun faint in haze —

By the road, little sign: 'Churches in Golden —
A, B, C —' Sure, there'd be little groups of people,
each in their own way … then remembered:
They aren't worshipping the mountains.

# How Was Calgary?

*for George Bowering*

Hard to tell. There were lots of golden lights, like golden
marbles, on a glass tray — but rising & falling — though some of
that apparent motion was due to the bus, & the rising & falling
of the land over which it was approaching — & then the subject
was in among the golden lights & saw they were — street lights
(aw, you guessed!) —

& amid all the golden lights, *Woody's RV World* — that was a
coincidence, S. reports, since he was thinking, what might count
as 'world' for an AI system, when that flashed by, & then later,
*Ristorante Ristorante*. Took him back to his youth, when even
the best Italian restaurant was called a restaurant, & that took
him back to all his talks with Stan, their never-ending conversation,
about how things had changed since their youth — *one* youth?

A consciousness — something — stretched out between the
past (seen as a kind of paradisal, happy-go-lucky place — a *real*
place, where you could eat spaghetti (& not linguini) — & not,
somehow, just be the focal point of a sketch — a schematic — of
the act of eating spaghetti — focal point — the fork, the mouth,
the throat — while level on level, at the same time, other voices
(other persons?) from this time & that, mumbled, muttered,
half-started phrases, the beginning of arguments you had to pay

attention to, & at the same time try not to pay attention to, try to
be real again —

this is what S. argued with Stan about, whether plain,
uncomplicated reality was disappearing or were they just getting
older — but why should getting older have that effect?

& it happening inside the head —

A man on a bus sees a sign from the window, *Woody's RV World*,
& can't understand it, because he's passing by it —

& then on Stephen Avenue, dressed for late winter, & this is
suddenly full spring — 5 PM — warm, with a light wind, but the
Calgarians have made this mistake too, dressed in topcoats,
anorak jackets (?) — it's 15° out, & you push open the thick glass
door of the Bankers Hall & are met with a puff of hot air — it's
20° inside, the heat is on in all the buildings —

so, of course, in 10 minutes (& why are there periods of time?),
at the bar, peering out of this flesh —

at 2 brokers (not lawyers, they seem too self-satisfied — maybe
auditors — bankers more likely) who *are* each other —

(right now there's some kind of a terrier — one of those square-
jawed fuzzy brown dogs — taking a shit behind a bush in the
central play area of the Econo Court — I like that name, Econo
Court) —

2 heads bald on top, expensive haircuts, one with a well-trimmed
beard (the only difference), suits, ties, cuffs, pints of Smithwick's

(this is an Irish pub, the James Joyce — how wonderful to be someone else, to *be* the person you are drinking with — & not a turmoil of voices, fear, memories, arguments, in the dark of this head — trying to be one person — to be real, i.e., not a person — if this is what it is to be a person, I can't imagine the other people — the bartenders in their black vests & Kelly green bow ties, the brokers — think, no, *are*, like this — lack of sympathy, I guess.

I'd like to drink pint after pint, each accompanied by a shooter of Jameson, & then for this reality to segue, imperceptibly, into some other — why, into the past, of course — the thoughts becoming more intermittent — but the scene getting sharper & brighter & clearer — though the *characters*, I guess, moving more slowly — until finally, no movement, no thought, just a bright image —

(of *justice*, he thinks, oddly)

rather than having to finish my drink (S. finishes his pint, pays up —

(now a St. Bernard romping, followed by a woman in blue slacks & what I guess is an anorak jacket — I'm not really sure — (but what I meant to report when I noted the other dog, the boxy-faced terrier — is that it's good to be here (that's a riff for Ryan), in Calgary. I have Mr. Coffee & it's only 8:15 AM & I have my whole life ahead of me) —

pays up, as I was saying, & goes back out onto Stephen Avenue, it's 5 to 7, still warm, light wind — & as he left the bar, no, just at the moment when he downed the last of the pint, placed the 25 bucks on the bill & the bartender smiled & said 'Have a nice evening,' just then he kind of shrugged all this off, all this interior stuff, & became, briefly, the person he is, as he does, intermittently, as he passed through the door, as he does, passing

✳

ristorante (This one is Gaston's Ristorante.)

✳

Sign in Eau Claire Market:

>
> MORE EXCITING
> SHOPS UPSTAIRS

✳

Why should a sign:

>
> Own a New
> Mercedes-Benz
> From $37,550

remind me that I'm going to die?

What is this 'reminding'?

✳

Why Not Italian Too! Ristorante

'Blondes on Bikes' boys waggling their hips at Burns Stadium — & then they stop, forever, when the social takes over from the physical, age 12. A non-sexual longing, for an age of bikes & baseball.

    Longing for the boys? no, sorry, boys for boys & baseball for the old — boys banging the corrugated steel fence at

the top of the grandstand — when the scoreboard says 'Make
Some Noise' — it makes a helluva racket. Cannons have a
chance — fight back from being behind 9-1 in the 5th to lead
15-14 going into the 9th but then Las Vegas scores 6 runs in the
top of the 9th —
                all this time a big bank of cloud coming slowly
out of the west as the evening darkens — the lights on — the
lights on also for some reason over McMahon Stadium across
the way, though there's no game going on there —

Consciousness is an illusion, a dear friend of Stan's & mine,
Jim Herndon, dead now these — what is it, 10 years? — said
Lévi-Strauss said — & that he agreed with him —

but Stephen Leacock replied (well, replied in my mind,
writing): 'The illusion is the real reality.'
                      The boys — & girls —
waggling their hips — dancing to the R&B — led by the
Cannons' mascot — red Sesame Street type creature — &
why do all mascots have wide hips? (you know what you can do
with your counterexamples) —
                    & remembering 4 years ago in
Syracuse, boys dancing to 'YMCA', making the letters with their
arms over their heads —
                but they won't play 'YMCA' in Calgary —
which is what Stan & I were arguing about — are we genetically
'homosexual' or do boys just stop waggling their hips when they
discover life is no longer joyous — age 12.

At age 12 I found out I was a 'homosexual' & stopped waggling
my hips.

✳

How was life? The illusion. 12 to 64.

S. tries to get behind his thoughts — his 'thoughts' I should say
— not sure that's what to call such powerful fragments —
'strings' of words flash across his cortex, I guess — or up & down
— of 'words' — I won't try to give examples — his private
lexicon — the crumbs he's taken home from all his parties,
hoping at first no one noticed —

Illusion, you call it? — illusion
stuck here — would like to be elsewhere, but the thoughts —

Some people think what's hard to explain about consciousness is
how well it works — ha! — tell that to the insomniac — tell it to
Blanche Dubois — with a song caught in her head — who's
singing that song?

stuck stuck stuck stuck stuck —

a sleeping Siberian tiger — a peregrine falcon — giraffe trying to
open the 20-ft. door with its head — gave up — then saw it out-
side with the other giraffe, so it must've — the elephant tried to
pick up nothing dragging the tip of its trunk along the spiky
fence — no pain sensors? or just dulled, by repetition?

'There is no first person in literature,' Wilde told Gide. There is
too much of a first person — & yet I know, just beyond this (blank)
of words is a country without reflection — a river (like the Bow)
that flows from the past to the present & makes them one — one
*place* — the second martini has that effect too — S. snaps back
into the landscape — ristorante-scape — & the landscape knows
its being — the less he knows the more it is aware —

The woman in black — first unsure if it was a woman — black hair, black jacket, black slacks — head in her hands, moaned, said something like, 'It's something else,' & then slid off her seat to the floor of the C-Train & lay at my feet, face down, moaning — & the 4 teenagers laughed & made a joke about heroin & then one of them went to the safety phone & pushed the red button & the green light came on & the teenager said, 'There's a woman lying on the floor of the train looks like she's OD'd or something,' & two other people came & knelt down by her & said, 'Are you all right?' & 'She's all right, she's breathing,' & Blanche Dubois watched them take care of her

& the sleeping Siberian tiger

content

# In Ireland

### 1   *The Dying Cow*

My father appeared to me, or rather,
appeared in me, as I was sitting at the bar
in a pub in Wicklow called The Dying Cow.
Appeared in me, shoulders in my shoulders,
lips in my lips, in that attitude
of resignation that marked his old age.

I realized I had long warded him off,
looked in the mirror countless times
& saw my short hair sticking up like his
      from my age-high brow
& quickly brushed it to the side;
felt my lips purse in that small mouth of his
that could not kiss (but admired kissing)
& more & more as he grew old would not
speak, knowing what he had to say would be
of no importance.
          I would be gay, I would
(pretend to) kiss. His anger, in childhood,
     had propelled me outward,
to seek a world where to be what he was not,
whatever that might be, might be wanted —
not learned, because I thought I had it in me —

some secret soul yet daunted by his look,
      by his repeated rebuke,
horrified that I might be that way.

How far I ran from him to discover a place
      (New York)
where I could finally begin. Combed my hair
to let it fall over my brow, widened, with effort,
my smile. Especially in snapshots.

I am trying to tell all this too quickly,
as if the right word (that might come to me
as I thought my soul would come to me
as a teenager, breaking away from him) might tell
some truth about us. About him & me.


2   *Coolgreany Wood*

Thoughts of death walking through old oak wood
much of which had been cut for furniture.
Look at a space between branches: no world,
nothing surrounding, clouds indifferent.

Odd affection for the openness of that sky —
Felt his co-presence sharp again within me —
This time it was the universe's turn
      to say nothing.

# Veracruz

In Veracruz, city of breezes & sailors & loud birds,
an old man, I walked the Malecón by the sea,

and I thought of my father, who when a young man
had walked the Malecón in Havana, dreaming of Brazil,

and I wished he had gone to Brazil
& learned magic,

and I wished my father had come back to San Francisco
armed with Brazilian magic, & that he had married
not my mother, but her brother, whom he truly loved.

I wish my father had, like Tiresias, changed himself into a
    woman,
& that he had been impregnated by my uncle, & given birth to me
    as a girl.

I wish that I had grown up in San Francisco as a girl,
a tall, serious girl,

& that eventually I had come to Veracruz,
& walking on the Malecón, I had met a sailor,
a Mexican sailor or a sailor from some other country —
    maybe a Brazilian sailor,
& that he had married me, & I had become pregnant
    by him,
so that I could give birth at last to my son — the boy
    I love.

# October (A Translation)

In the beginning, there was more divinity in a bestial or simply enigmatic idol than in a human image.

No tree exists before the word 'tree,' but only that which will become a tree.

My dog obeys the slightest whiff of scent more than my word.

Spring like a fever & Fall like death throes. In between, the painful, wasteful sickness of Summer.

Violent rain beats down the dahlias in the garden; already sick with the Fall, brown-edged & softened by frost, they begin to rot.

When we feel strongly about things, we think we get closer to them. But what happens when we experience things normally, or with indifference or boredom, that is, without giving anything of ourselves?

The world, outside, inside, is a violent contradiction. Only split in two can one live thoroughly.

The body, minus the I, belongs to reality. It touches reality absolutely, as a body, in the absolute darkness of the body. Touches reality without me.

Neither sea nor desert is 'landscape.'

A place is only sacred when men take it over, in the limited way they can. When it lends itself to that purpose, it is marked off.

The appearance of things is in us only, not in the things.

The real is not unknowable. It is *real*.

We can be reassured only by ourselves.

The world is bound to its mystery. Bound like a leaf to a twig. Fastened so, freely, as to its source, its basis. And the attachment is seamless.

One says almost nothing to others. One just talks. And from this monologue, each takes what he needs, even at times in an opposite sense.

Things are only half understood. But to get even that far requires great care.

The world is only there to tell its story, one which begins with it and follows it closely, but is not the world.

My poem lacks continuity. It is made of dispersed moments, flashes at intervals.

Enclosures, fences, hedges, walls. A man can only breathe behind doors.

Life is moisture. At the same time, it is fire, the drying of moisture.

The rain falls outside, tireless & cold, as if beyond it, nothing would ever happen.

Words arise by themselves, when speech is necessary. Where do they come from?

That the world has meaning in no other way than by being the world, that it might tell a different story & yet be the same, that is its glory & its passion.

Am I the one who will die, or just an old man?

I tried to express a thought, but I didn't know how to say it. So it was really no thought.

What oppresses us has no voice. It dominates only by not speaking.

Perhaps it prevails only by its silence.

The silence of stones is a freshness, less muffled than hardened. Inaudible & hardened.

Death is the only exit from the real. This is its horror. Have mercy.

Not to speak of the wind, but to be pierced by the wind to the point of speaking.

The Adversary is silent. Is there even an adversary, if it is silent? Is it, because it is silent, no adversary?

There are not two ways of being. No one has more than his own.

That of another is not, cannot be, a way of *being*. Nothing more than a possible …

The world made itself, it still makes itself before our eyes, without knowledge. So we should do, or try to do, what we can, without knowledge.

The low clouds are also the nearest sky. Down here below.

'Oblivion! How sweet this word is,' sighed Joubert.

It's obvious: all that rises comes from below.

Wrapped in sadness, as in a deaf wave, almost dreaming.

All that burns shines. And all that shines burns.

What I am trying to say, you cannot hear, unless you join me in the zone of shadow.

Late twilight, when one can see only after first getting used to the shadow.

Will the animals know of this misfortune?

The rays of the evening sun do no more than record that they are light.

The evening is beautiful, undeciphered.

*Adapted from the French of Roger Munier*
*through the Spanish of Aurelia Álvarez Urbajtel*

# Safeco Field, Seattle, August 22, 1999

*for Gerald & George*

Screw All Fans Except Corporate Owners!

Just like in Syracuse & Calgary,
young boys are dancing here, artlessly,
on the steep steps of the upper deck,

& one-beered young men,
bare-chested, with incipient love handles,
punch the air, & push their hips

forward. They can see themselves

magnified, on the big RealTime screen,
in centre field, next to the scoreboard,
& turned on by their lusty images, they bump into each other,
& dance & punch harder,

till some Master of Revels at a split-screen monitor
pans away from them
to someone else cute or funny.

Meanwhile, far beneath us, in miniature,
Seattle & Cleveland baseball players
(both, incongruously, wearing blue 'away' shirts)
run & slide, throw & catch
in patterns that seem controlled
by the flight of the tiny, bright ball:
a perfect simulacrum.

The 'wave' sweeps across the crowd. Section by section,
the fans stand up & sit down. George says,
'In Seattle, they don't know the 'wave' was over
          years ago.'

Are the young men dancing for their images?
Are their images dancing for them?
If asked, might some of them
not want to change places
with their RealTime doubles,

& stay virtual, dancing
& safe, at Safeco Field?

# Vancouver, Book One

### 1

There is more here than memory.

Reading *Paterson* on the bus, back & forth. Across the city. The 210. A man & a city.

I am not a man & this is not my city.

Williams though as a guide. His universals as particulars, ideas in things. His rhythms. Ever rhythmic, shaking (like a belly-dancer), splashing (like the Falls) lines. Insistences. Insistence on persisting. Oh, maybe that, yes. But to take the thing to its — or maybe come back & find it later. Seasonal. Recurrences. And something else 'out of the blue' with a certainty (but I have no certainty) that the fact of it ('of it,' that's Williams) — might —

Vertigo. Vair to go?

(Student comes up to my desk with woeful expression. 'I forgot to double space. Should I start over?' 'No. Double space now.')

Reading him back & forth on the bus, the 210, & also reading

him forth, & then back, back to the beginning of some 'poem'
— in the long poem, some break, impetus — of thought — &
perception — pent up, while it seems *he* is *reading* the prose
passages he has written, reading ahead, reading a newspaper,
or in the library, page of an almanac, memoir, time before his
childhood, turns the page —

& his mind takes off, & so much of it (there's that 'of it' again
— lost it there — students handing in papers) — somewhere
there's coloured petals (paper after paper lights on the pile) —
or something like fruits, flowers, lights, held up, & dancing in
the fountain — they come from everywhere — & this is the
point — from anywhere — the *it* is large enough — you see,
it's all —

Watching it go by on the bus, even — that's relativity — I mean
watching me go by — the city. I imagine a poem about
Vancouver in which Vancouver never appears — no, I mean *no
glimpses* — Vancouver only in the mind of — trying to let it be,
thinking that if (& what about the subject position? that revealed
coyly, or just blurted out?) Thinking that if — no glimpses, but
the first thing glimpsed would open the way for (some idea of
rubble here, rubbies?) — the way — the diagonal — / the tracks /
— extending from the CP main line (careful, watch it!) through
Gastown, across Hastings at Carrall (this is like Saint-Henri in
*The Tin Flute*, train tracks crossing the people's street — an
account of all (oh, some) of the many times, ways, this (subject
position) crossed, or stayed on the same side of the street (coyly,
letting no one know who he was), or crossed & disappeared into
Army & Navy, beginning that catalogue, rubble — or

V is for Victory Square — *Is It Nothing To You* — glimpsed first I
guess on a pub crawl, with Dennis Forkin & Evert Hoogers —

(Something about 'The Masses' — an institutional sign high on the wall of Army & Navy. I phoned up the head office. I was trying to sell them an ad in the *Grape* — I made some reference to that sign — the guy said, 'Aw, that was put up years ago' — disclaimed — any connection — to 'The Masses'

(When did they — cease to be? Timothy Garton Ash saw them in Budapest around 1990 — they were funny-looking — big noses, faces that bulged — they didn't all look the same — coats & ties on workers) —

Pub crawls started on Main ('In all the beer parlors, all down along Main Street'). It feels like it would be Saturday morning — in the Fall — start of the school year — denial of that — transgression. The American, the Cobalt (dyke) — & there was one in Chinatown, too, was it Pender & Gore? — & then back down Pender & around the corner onto Hastings. One glass (20¢) or small (10¢) at each —

Stuck stuck stuck the W — a poem in the new *Sulfur* began with a quote from Bréton that the surrealists opposed the W to the V of the visible —

The W atop Woodward's — the big, brick, block-long (almost — next building west was Woolworth's — another W (west a W, was a W) — the Food Floor — little restaurant behind, lunch counter (like where Florentine worked) — the polished oak framed glass doors — 2 sets — a vestibule — or just a space between — push, to open — dark on Cordova — my fear, or anxiety, at winter — getting older, but that's — not adequate — snow — yes, but don't try to describe — feelings — the Parkade across the street — now empty — Woodward's boarded up — a big development sign — black on white — a placard, with a

diagram of the block — too high to read, to deter graffiti — &
warnings of dogs. Then the windows — Christmas displays —
angels twirling on canes & animals' mouths opened — did the
Bay take them — are they the same ones (I hear Margaret
Laurence's voice in that 'same') — & the snow & so many old
people, some bent over, carrying shopping bags — always some
kind of avoidance
    not to be a man,
    to be a thought
struggling through snow, carrying — not to care about the
meaning — plod
      stuck stuck stuck what kind of feeling down in
Woodward's basement on a Saturday morning buying fresh
ground peanut butter, then a cup of soup & a toasted tuna & a
Coke, sitting at the counter — the women in their uniforms —
brown & tan — did — word by word — plod — safety — always
felt in the past —

Upstairs buying pants, I said to the tailor, 'The woman was
showing me a pair,' & he (by the racks of pants) said, 'She's a
lady' — emphasizing *his* past, gentility — & I'm trying to drag
him back into an earlier past — well only slightly earlier —
'The Masses' —

Still in that space between the doors — of Woodward's. Back
door, steps coming down from the main floor, or up from the
basement — the Food Floor. Polished oak frames of the doors —
glass. Warm in here, looking out at the snow — there are hard
rubber mats attached to the hardwood floor — to knock the
snow off — wet snow falling fast in streaks, against the darkness.
The dark shape of the Parkade, across the street, filled with cars
(now empty). Waiting for — feeling safe — image of finger to
lips as if something not to be said. Stuck stuck stuck stuck stuck

stuck stuck the pub crawl goes by on the other side of the —
trying too hard to think — store — Hastings — the W rises on its
little Eiffel Tower — the W seen from the other side of the inlet
— red, turning slowly — from the Seabus — turn-of-the-century
façade of warehouses — feelings without words about places —

like driving (so many times) from Berkeley across the Bay Bridge
to SF in the early evening — Friday — & seeing the lights going
on up the streets on Nob Hill — red & blue spots of cocktail bars
at the corners — & thinking, there's something there for me —
there's life —

but this is different, I'm almost cowering in the space between
the doors of Woodward's — afraid to go out — as if some terrible
thing, some terror, was coming (& not assuming any knowledge)
over the city, low buildings to the west, behind the snow — that
to go out would be
                    the beginning of knowing this city

& the different Canadians, their minds, that patience, waiting
for me to finish (as now) my account of what it was like.

That's finished, that's what it was like, now let's have supper.
Lamps from second-hand stores. A different sense of time, of
events, here, as discrete, not overlapping.

But out there in the night, other. Other than being here, in the
city. And close.

And outer.

2

The W

turned against the sky
like a reminder
of people of people

The W

turned against the sky, impersonal
reminder of a certain way of life, people
envisioning people, not merely plural

Like the Lions, & like the twin piles
of sulfur on the North Shore

The W

turned in the air like an X-
mas star, a reminder
of people as people

(like the hills of sulfur mean nothing
except that it falls so (we fall so)

like the Lions (up the canyon)
are rock as human

But the people as people
thronging the streets, post-war
in search not so much of luxuries
as of attractive (or acceptable) necessities
to continue
living in a golden age,

as it seems now to us
knowing it was not to you.

You gave it authority,
though it crippled you.

My students,
thinking us '60s softies hard
on them, but soft on us,
on our own style of idleness,
know neither of our
displacement
nor of your devotion.

Crossing Burrard Inlet
& passing between
mountainous freighters
& cyclopean sea-cranes

The W
            turned,
                        turned against the sky
like a reminder of people of people.

Turned against life, against death,
against mortality, eternity,
turned, turned.

(& in this era of vegetarian pizza,
disappearance of the Government, & of the People)

※

Like the Lions, before I came,
ran out on the field
to roar in '54
at Empire Stadium
where Roger Bannister & John Landy ran the mile.

The W
        wasn't turning,
                wasn't
there.

'The Woodward's Beacon was a 2 million candlepower rotating
searchlight perched on an Eiffel Tower-like structure built atop
Woodward's department store in 1927. The beam from this well-
known landmark could be seen from as far away as Chilliwack.
In the late 1950s the light was replaced by its present 5-metre (16
foot) high, red neon 'W.''

Not like the Q,
the swizzle stick at the Quay,
or Park Royal,
'Becoming more like you
every day.'

✳

I have a vision of
a place, light shifting,
night & day, where Earle Birney's
'Vancouver Lights' is read
down
from the North Shore
into a bottomless pit.

*

The W turned
towards the sky,
the depths of the sky

The hills of sulfur
mean nothing
except that we fall so

The Lions are human rock,
wanting
to move forward, to prance

*

As Landy & Bannister
are men of bronze

human bronze

as Bannister passed Landy
that day

Landy & Bannister were of us
(who wrote that, 'of us'?)

'Bannister shot past Landy'
(not to my knowledge, I was someone else,
a soldier in Arkansas)

& Terry Fox

was of us

& Steve Fonyo
at least
is not postmodern

✳

Who were we?
The ones that got dirty
or, fanatically, stayed clean

(But we all got 'dressed up'
to go downtown
on the cars, on Saturday)
Who were we?

✳

They have to shop
at the Chinese stores
where they can't read the language
since the Food Floor closed

# Notes

THE PUCK    '*Cliffs of fall*': See Gerard Manley Hopkins, 'No worst, there is none.' Barry: Barry McKinnon. See *The Centre* (Prince George: Caitlin, 1995). Another version of this poem was included in *Gentle Northern Summer* (Vancouver: New Star, 1995).

THE WASTELAND    For the French text, see Arkadi Tcherkassov, 'Onze histoires vécues sur 'l'amitié des peuples' dans la vie courante' (tr. Lionel Meney). *Cité Libre* (Montreal) 22:5 (Sept.-Oct. 1994).

TERRACE '79    Peter Weber, Allen Gottesfeld, Ian Anderson, and Dora FitzGerald were instructors at Northwest Community College.

AUBADE    In line 2, *The East Village Poetry Web* changed 'odor' to 'door.' I liked it.

THE RIPPLE    Originally included in *The Stick* (Vancouver: Talonbooks, 1974).

AT ANDY'S    GB: George Bowering. Barry: Barry McKinnon. 'come in late, like Ken Belford': See *Sign Language* (Prince George: Repository-Gorse, 1979).

OCTOBER    For the Spanish text, see Roger Munier, 'Octubre' (tr. Aurelia Álvarez Urbajtel). *Vuelta* (Mexico City) 241 (Dec. 1996). 'Down here below': This is the title of a song by Abbey Lincoln. Joubert: Joseph Joubert, French diarist (1754-1824). In the afterword to *The Notebooks of Joseph Joubert* (ed. & tr. Paul Auster, San Francisco: North Point, 1983), Maurice Blanchot quotes Joubert: 'I would like thoughts to succeed one another in a book like stars in the sky, with order, with harmony, but effortlessly and at intervals, without touching, without mingling ...'

VANCOUVER, BOOK ONE    *The Tin Flute*: Gabrielle Roy's 1945 novel. Florentine: the main character in the novel. 'The Woodward's Beacon ...': Bruce Macdonald, *Vancouver: A Visual History* (Vancouver: Talonbooks, 1992).

# Acknowledgments

*Blue Canary* (Milwaukee), *It's Still Winter* (on line), *rout/e* (Vancouver), *Sal Mimeo* (New York), *Tads* (Vancouver), *The Capilano Review* (North Vancouver), *The East Village Poetry Web* (on line).